SHORT CI[RCULAR] WAL[KS] IN THE YORKSHIRE DALES
Vol. 1 - Southern area.

by

JOHN N. MERRILL

Maps and photographs by John N. Merrill

TRAIL CREST PUBLICATIONS Ltd.,
- "from footprint to finished book."

1993

Sandia Mountains
New Mexico. USA

**TRAIL CREST PUBLICATIONS Ltd.,
WINSTER, MATLOCK, DERBYSHIRE. DE4 2DQ**
☎ **(0629) 826354**
FAX **(0629) 826354**

This book is copyright under the Berne Convention. All rights are reserved. Apart from any fair dealing for the purposes of private study, research, criticism or review, as permitted under the Copyright Act, 1956, no part of this publication may be reproduced, stored in a retrieval system, or transmitted in any other form by any means, electronic, electrical, chemical, mechanical, optical, photocopying, recording or otherwise, without the prior permission of the copyright owner. Enquiries should be addressed to the publishers.

Concieved, edited, typeset, designed, paged, printed, marketed and distributed by John N. Merrill.

© Text & walks - John N. Merrill 1993
© Maps & photographs - John N. Merrill 1993.

First Published - February 1993

ISBN 1 874754 06 3

Please note - The maps in this guide are purely illustrative. You are encouraged to use the appropriate 1:25,000 O.S. map.

*U.S.A. office -
P.O.Box 124.
Santa Rosa,
New Mexico.
88435
U.S.A.*

Meticulous research has been undertaken to ensure that this publication is highly accurate at the time of going to press. The publishers, however, cannot be held responsible for alterations, errors or omissions, but they would welcome notification of such for future editions.

Typeset in - Bookman bold, italic and plain 9pt and 18pt.

Printed by - John N. Merrill at Milne House, Speedwell Mill, Miller's Green, Wirksworth, Derbyshire. DE4 4BL

Cover sketch "Dry Valley near Malham Cove"
by John Creber - © Trail Crest Publications Ltd. 1993.

An all British product.

The author on the summit of Mt.Taylor (11,301ft.), New Mexico.

ABOUT JOHN N. MERRILL

Born in the flatlands of Bedfordshire he soon moved to Sheffield and discovered the joy of the countryside in the Peak District, where he lives. A keen walker who travels the world exploring mountains and trails. Over the last twenty years he has walked more than 150,000 miles and worn out over sixty pairs of boots. He has written more than 120 walk guides to areas in Britain and abroad, and created numerous challenge walks which have been used to raise more than £500,000 for charity. New Mexico, USA is his second home.

CONTENTS

Page No.

ABOUT JOHN N. MERRILL 3
INTRODUCTION 5
ABOUT THE WALKS 7
GRIMWITH RESERVOIR - 4 MILES 8
KILNSEY CRAG - 2 1/2 MILES 10
STAINFORTH & CATRIGG FORCE - 3 MILES 12
BORDLEY - 5 MILES 14
MALHAM COVE - 5 MILES 16
GRASSINGTON - 5 MILES 18
APPLETREEWICK - 4 1/2 MILES 20
AIRTON - 4 1/2 MILES 22
WINTERBURN - 5 1/2 MILES 24
RYLSTONE - 6 1/2 MILES 26
HOWGILL & SIMON'S SEAT - 4 MILES 28
FLASBY & SHARP HAW - 357m - 6 MILES 30
BOLTON PRIORY - 7 1/2 MILES 32
EMBSAY MOOR RESERVOIR & CRAG - 3 1/2 MILES 34
SETTLE & ATTERMIRE SCAR - 5 MILES 36
BEAMSLEY BEACON, 393m. - 2 MILES 38
LEEDS & LIVERPOOL CANAL - 3 WALKS 40
WALK RECORD CHART 42
WALK BADGE ORDER FORM 43
OBSERVE THE COUNTRY CODE 44
THE HIKERS CODE 45
EQUIPMENT NOTES 46
OTHER BOOKS BY JOHN MERRILL 47

INTRODUCTION

The Yorkshire Dales are an outstanding walking area. The southern area is very diverse with such majestic limestone features of Malham Cove, Gordale Scar and Kilnsey Crag. Traversing the area is the beautiful River Wharfe. While in the eastern side are gritstone outcrops and moors. From my boarding school in Harrogate we often had school camps near Patley Bridge, from where I was initiated into walking and the Dales.

Walking the area again for this guide I have striven to illustrate the wide variety of walks that are to be found in the southern area. From peaceful river walks to high moorland. All have their own character and uniqueness. Where possible the walks start from a car park and include an inn enroute; some tearooms. They are all circular but with options to explore further. Whilst I have attempted to give full information you are advised to carry the appropriate 1:25,000 map to get the best out of the area.

Here then are some of my favourite walks in the southern part of The Dales. Further volumes will cover the other areas of the National Park. May I wish you *Happy walking*, and may the sun always shine!

John N. Merrill. 1993

Limestone pavement above Malham Cove.

Bolton Priory and the River Wharfe.

Whilst every care is taken detailing and describing the walk in this book, it should be borne in mind that the countryside changes by the seasons and the work of man. I have described the walk to the best of my ability, detailing what I have found on the walk in the way of stiles and signs. Obviously with the passage of time stiles become broken or replaced by a ladder stile or even a small gate. Signs too have a habit of being broken or pushed over. All the route follow rights of way and only on rare occasions will you have to overcome obstacles in its path, such as a barbed wire fence or electric fence. On rare occasions rights of way are rerouted and these ammendments are included in the next edition.

The seasons bring occasional problems whilst out walking which should also be borne in mind. In the height of summer paths become overgrown and you will have to fight your way through in a few places. In low lying areas the fields are often full of crops, and although the pathline goes straight across it may be more practical to walk round the field edge to get to the next stile or gate. In summer the ground is generally dry but in autumn and winter, especially because of our climate, the surface can be decidedly wet and slippery; sometimes even gluttonous mud!

These comments are part of countryside walking which help to make your walk more interesting or briefly frustrating. Standing in a farmyard up to your ankles in mud might not be funny at the time but upon reflection was one of the highlights of the walk!

The mileage for each walk is based on three calculations -

1. pedometer reading.
2. the route map measured on the map.
3. the time I took for the walk.

I believe the figure stated for each walk to be very accurate but we all walk differently and not always in a straight line! The time allowed for each walk is on the generous side and does not include pub stops etc. The figure is based on the fact that on average a person walks 2 1/2 miles an hours but less in hilly terrain.

GRIMWITH RESERVOIR
- 4 MILES

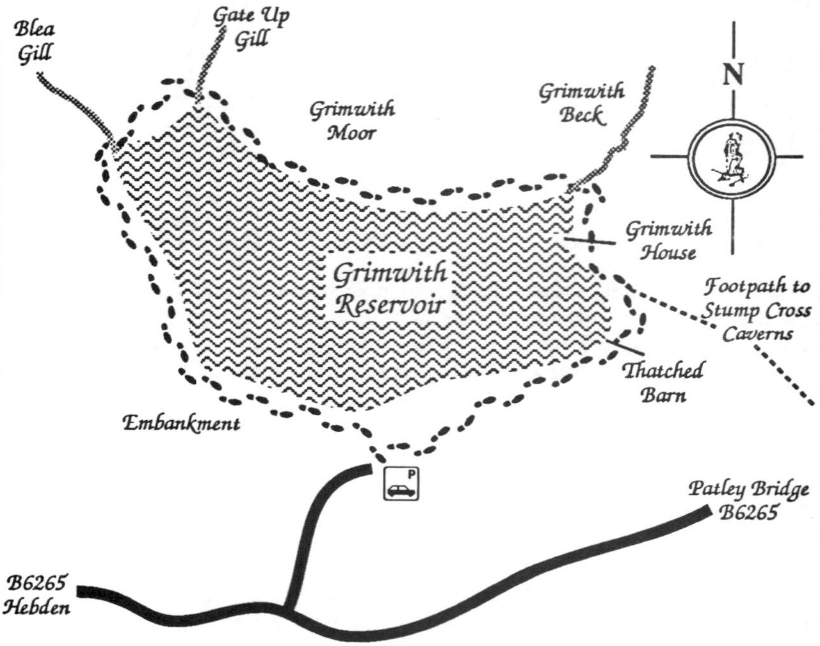

Thatched barn and Grimwith Reservoir.

GRIMWITH RESERVOIR - 4 MILES
- allow 1 1/2 hours.

🚶 🚶 🚶 - *Car park - Waterside path - Grimwith Beck - Gate Up Gill - Embankment - Car park.*

The walk can be extended by 2 miles by following the path to Stump Cross Caverns - return same way.

 1:25,000 Outdoor Leisure Map No. 10 - Yorkshire Dales - southern area.

- *Overlooking reservoir - Grid Ref. 063640.*

🍷- *None on the walk - nearest in Hebden, 3 miles to the west.*

ABOUT THE WALK - A beautiful walk, walking anti-clockwise around the reservoir, surrounded by impressive moorland. I saw many birds as I walked round one fine spring morning, including a Canada Geese with four chicks.

WALKING INSTRUCTIONS - Turn right from the car park along the track to a gate and stile. Just after turn left at a footpath sign - Waterside Path - and descend nearer to the water's edge. In 1/4 mile reach a track close to an impressive thatched building and turn left along it. In a few yards on your right is the path and sign for Stump Cross Cavern a mile away. Continue on the path/track encircling the reservoir, pass Grimwith House and Grimwith Beck and a mile later a ruined building on your left. 1/2 mile later cross the bridge over Gate Up Gill - the remotest part. 1/4 mile later cross Blea Gill and walk along the west side of the reservoir. Less than 1/2 mile later turn left as footpath signed - Across Barn Embankment. At the end of the embankment ascend back to the car park.

KILNSEY CRAG - 2 1/2 MILES

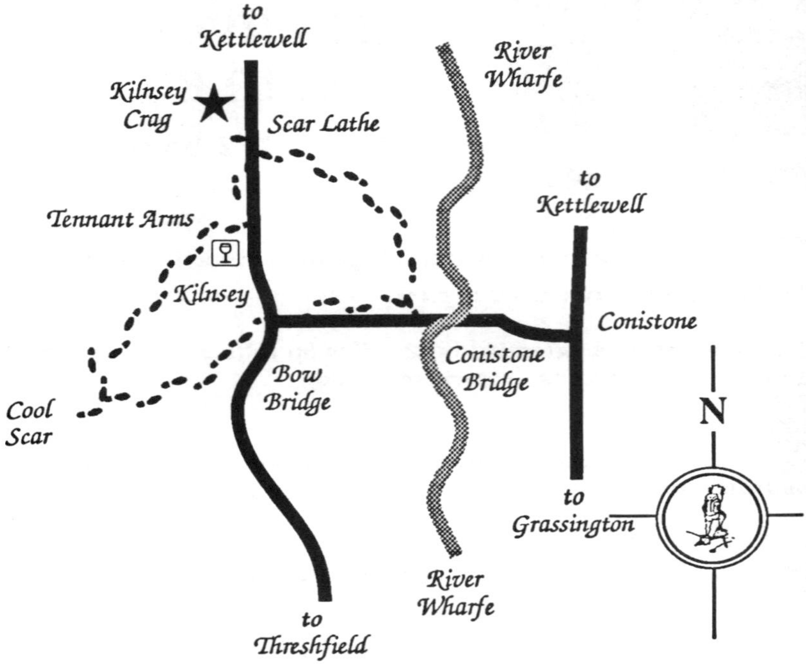

Kilnsey Crag.

KILNSEY CRAG
- 2 1/2 MILES
- allow 1 hour.

🚶🚶🚶 - *Conistone Bridge - B6160 - Kilnsey Crag - Tennant Arms - Cool Scar - Bow Bridge - Conistone Bridge.*

 1:25,000 Outdoor Leisure Map No. 10 - Yorkshire Dales - Southern area.

- *None. Very limited roadside parking around Conistone Bridge.*

🍷- *Tennant Arms, Kilnsey.*

ABOUT THE WALK - Outstanding! The overhanging limestone rock face of Kilnsey Crag is a masterpiece of nature. Today you see several climbers working their way up the face and overhang. The walk takes you across the fields to it and onto an inn before ascending to Cool Scar and the descent to Conistone Bridge. The nearby Kilnsey Aquarium & Angling centre is well worth a visit.

WALKING INSTRUCTIONS - From the western side of Conistone Bridge, over the River Wharfe, turn right at the gate and footpath sign - Scar Lathe. The path heads north then bears left to Scar Lathe, 1/2 mile away opposite Kilnsey Crag. Gaining the B6160 road here turn left to the Tennant Arms and turn right up the road "Unsuitable for Motorists." The tarmaced road soon swings left as you ascend towards the limestone escarpment - Cool Scar. In just over 1/4 mile keep left on the footpath signed track - Malham 5 1/2 miles. 200 yards along here beneath Cool Scar go through a stile by a gate on your left and descend to a footbridge and barn. Here gain a track and descend gently to Bow Bridge and the B6160 road. Turn left then right to Conistone Bridge and Conistone.

STAINFORTH & CATRIGG FORCE - 3 MILES

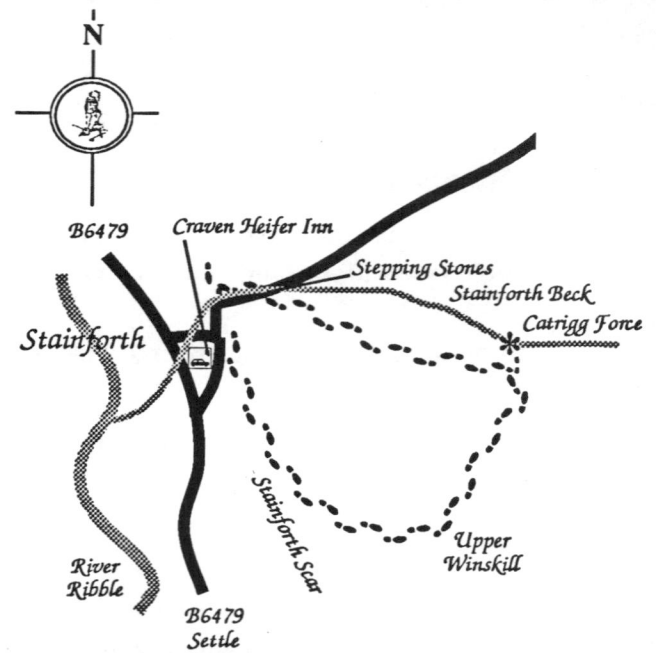

Stepping stones - Stainforth.

STAINFORTH & CATRIGG FORCE - 3 MILES
- allow 1 1/4 hours.

· · · - Stainforth - Stainforth Scar - Upper Winskill - Catrigg Force - Stainforth.

 1:25,000 Outdoor Leisure Map - No. 10 - Yorkshire Dales - Southern area.

 Central Stainforth.

- Craven Heifer, Stainforth.

ABOUT THE WALK - A delightful short walk up over a limestone scar to a tumbling waterfall - Catrigg Force. You return along a lane and cross stepping stones back into Stainforth.

WALKING INSTRUCTIONS - Turn right out of the car park and in a few yards right again. Just after the Craven Heifer Inn turn left at the footpath sign - Winskill. Ascend the gentle path for 1/4 mile to a kissing gate. Go through this and ascend to the top of the Stainforth Scar and a ladder stile. Walk along the top a short distance before turning left across the fields to the righthand side of Upper Winskill. Turn left along the track with the wall on your left, signposted Catrigg Force - 1/3 mile. Continue on the track and meeting another in 1/4 mile bear left along it to a gate. Almost opposite is the path down to Catrigg Force. Descend and see the force and retrace your steps. Turn right and descend the track/lane back to Stainforth 1/2 mile away. Entering the village bear right and cross the stepping stones over Stainforth Beck and turn left along the road. Follow it round to your left then turn right back to the car park.

Catrigg Force.

BORDLEY - 5 MILES

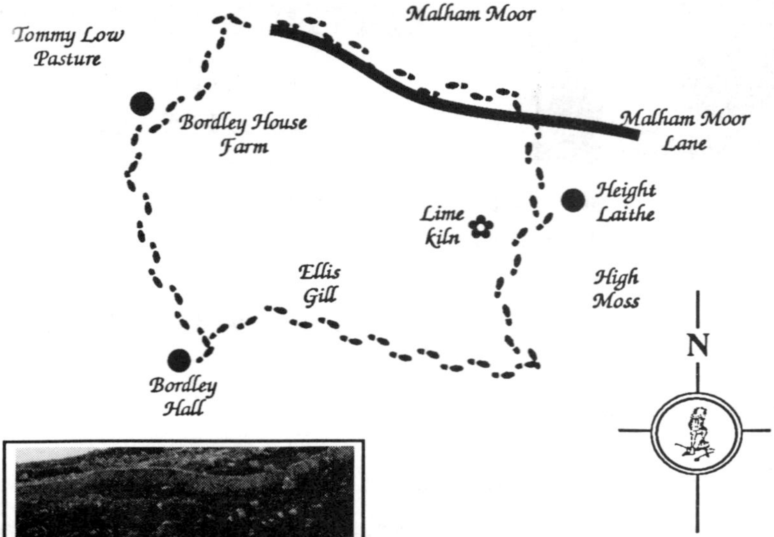

Lime kiln.

Bordley House Farm.

BORDLEY
- 5 MILES
- allow 2 hours.

🐾 *- Malham Moor Lane - Bordley - Bordley Hall - Ellis Gill - High Moss - Height Laithe - Malham Moor Lane.*

- 1:25,000 Outdoor Leisure Map No. 10 - Yorkshire Dales - Southern area.

- None. Roadside parking on Malham Moor Lane. Grid Ref. 950655.

- None - nearest in Threshfield 4 miles east.

ABOUT THE WALK - High remote walking on the limestone plateau to remote farms and where only the skylarks and curlew break the silence.

WALKING INSTRUCTIONS - Starting from the end of the tarmaced surface of Malham Moor Lane. Go through the gate and continue ahead on the track for a few yards before turning left, as signed - Bridleway - Bordley 1/2 mile. Descend the track and at a gate bear right for Bordley House Farm, dated 1818. Walk past the house and in a few yards turn left to a gate and follow the track beyond to another gate. At the end of the next field, where the track turns right keep ahead with the wall on your right to a stile. Now descending gain a gate and descend more steeply to another and Bordley Hall just beyond. Here the path sign states - Bordley Town 1/2 miles (where you have come from) and Bordley Road 1/4 mile. Turn left and cross a ford and ascend the track to a footpath junction 1/4 mile away, with a small plantation on your left. Cross the track to a gate and footpath sign - Boss Moor 1 1/2 miles. Follow a track across Ellis Gill and across a large field to a ladder stile. At the end of the next field gain a gate and walled track. Turn left and follow this bridlepath for 1/2 mile to Height Laithe. On your left is a lime kiln. Continue on the track above Height Laithe and in 1/4 mile reach Malham Moor Lane. Turn left along it back to your start.

MALHAM COVE, GORDALE SCAR & MALHAM TARN - 5 MILES

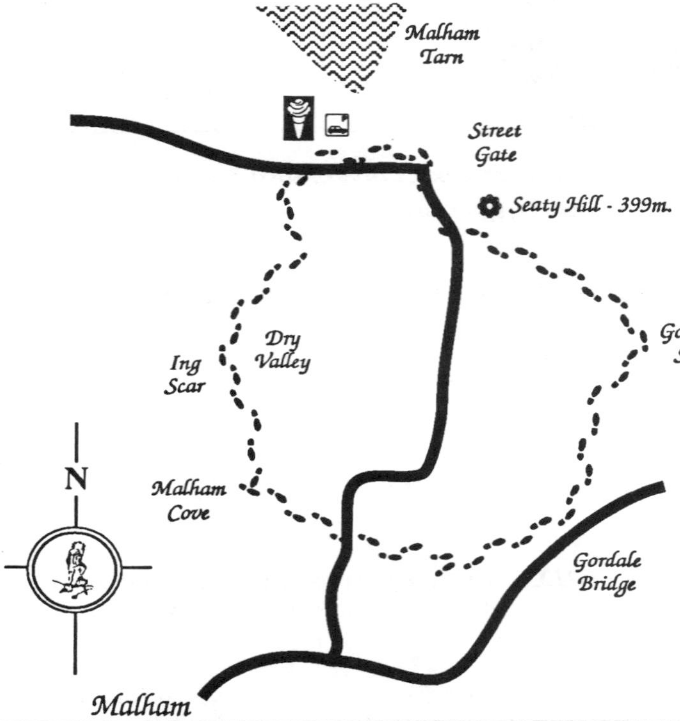

Gordale Scar.

MALHAM COVE, GORDALE SCAR & MALHAM TARN - 5 MILES

- allow 2 hours.

- Malham Tarn - Ing Scar - Malham Cove - Sheriff Hill - Gordale Bridge - Gordale Scar - Seaty Hill - Street Gate - Malham Tarn.

- 1:25,000 Outdoor Leisure Map No. 10 - Yorkshire Dales - Southern area.

- South of Malham Tarn on minor road at Grid Ref. 895658.

- None. Ice cream van at car park during the summer.

ABOUT THE WALK - Must rate as one of the finest in Britain, never mind the dales! I first came to Gordale Scar when few people were around, today you have to queue to ascend the rocky slab beside the fall, but this does not lessen the enjoyment of a magnificent day out. Simply set off and enjoy a superb walk in limestone scenery - they don't come any better!

WALKING INSTRUCTIONS - On the south side of the road on the right of the car park is a kissing gate. Go through here and in a few yards turn left as footpath signed - Malham Cove 1 1/2 miles. After 200 yards bear right on the path - Dry Valley & Malham Cove 1 mile - its been a quick 1/2 mile! The path keeps beside a wall before descending to the dry valley - cover sketch - and Ing Scar. Follow the path to the top of Malham Cove. On your left is a ladder stile. Cross this and bear right on the Pennine Way. Where it turns left keep ahead with a wall on your right and start descending gently keeping right to reach another ladder stile and minor road. Walk down the road a few yards to a stile on your left and path sign - Gordale 3/4 mile. the path descends and curves round to your left to a gate and onto a ladder stile. After this keep a wall on your left and gain the minor road near Gordale Bridge. Turn left and in a few yards left again and walk up the path into Gordale Scar. Follow it into the limestone walls and climb the rock scramble on the left of the waterfall. Continue ascending on a good path to the crest of the dale and stile. Continue on the path to a cairn and 1/2 mile later gain the minor road near Seaty Hill. Turn right along it and follow it round to your left back to the car park little over 1/2 mile away with views to Malham Tarn. Now for an ice-cream!

GRASSINGTON, GRASS WOOD & RIVER WHARFE - 5 MILES

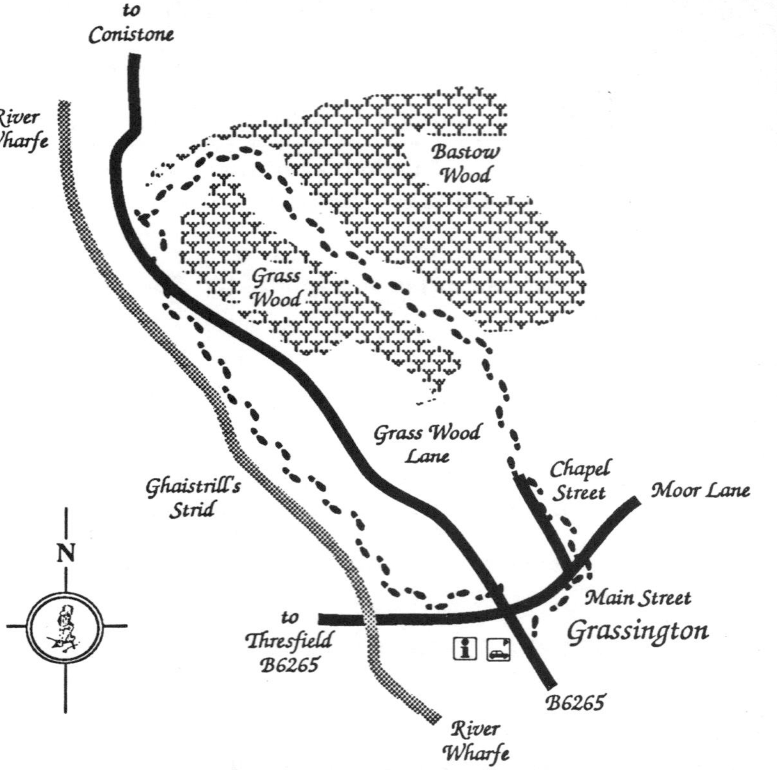

River Wharfe.

GRASSINGTON, GRASS WOOD & RIVER WHARFE
- 5 MILES
- allow 2 hours.

Grassington - Grass Wood - Conistone Road - River Wharfe - Ghaistrill's Strid - Grassington.

1:25,000 Outdoor Leisure map No. 10 - Yorkshire Dales - Southern area.

- Beside Information Centre on B6265 road. Grid Ref. 003638.

- Several in Grassington and numerous tearooms.

ABOUT THE WALK - First you walk through the bustling village before gaining the solitude of Grass Wood. After two miles you descend towards the River Wharfe and people! However the river path back to Grassington is incomparable and in beautiful weather is matchless.

WALKING INSTRUCTIONS - Turn left out of the car park then right along the Main Street - following a segment of the Dales Way. At the Town Hall turn left along Chapel Street, keeping to the left of Townhead. Just after is the Dales Way sign - Conistone. Continue a few more yards to the next path sign - Grass Wood and bear left to a gate. Continue on the track curving around to the wood and crossing limestone pavement. In less than 1/2 mile enter Grass Wood and keep heading north-westerly along the path/track for the next 3/4 mile; approximately half-way along pass a wall on your right. Gaining sparse woodland turn left on a distinct path, ascending a few yards before descending and in less than 1/4 mile you are on a good track on the northern edge of the wood. 1/4 mile later reach a stile and the minor road from Conistone - Grass Wood Lane. Turn left and 1/4 mile along here turn right through a kissing gate and follow the signed path - Grassington Bridge. Keep the River Wharfe on your right - first you are high above it - before walking along its banks to the bridge 1 1/2 miles away. En route passing Ghaistrill's Strid. Reaching the B6265 road - Station Road - turn left and ascend to central Grassington and turn right back to the Information Centre and car park.

APPLETREEWICK - 4 1/2 MILES

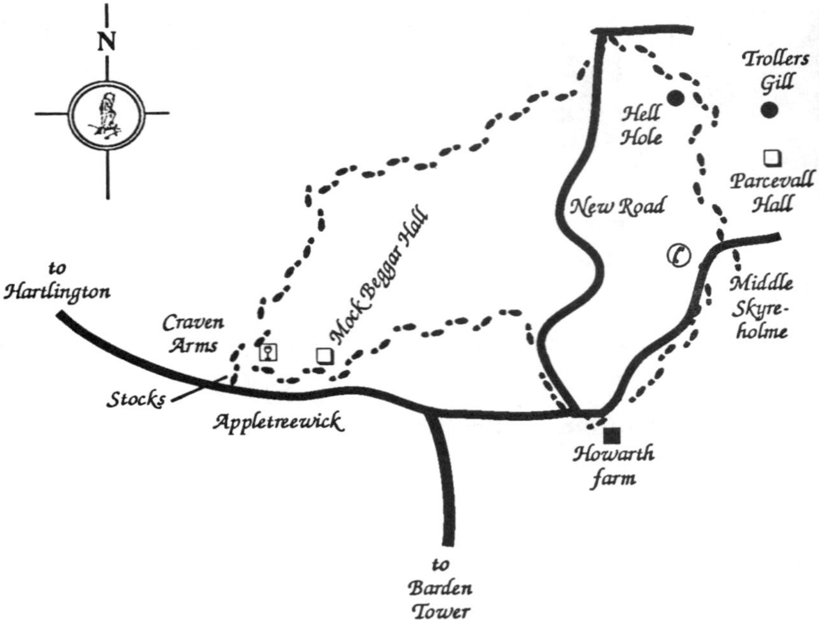

Skyreholme Beck.

from opposite page -

4 miles. Follow the track for 3/4 mile, crossing stiles and a ladder stile to a footpath/track junction. Turn left - signed Appletreewick. Follow the track around the field edges and over the hill and down to Appletreewick, gaining the road by the stocks and Craven Arms! Turn left to central Appletreewick.

APPLETREEWICK
- 4 1/2 MILES
- allow 2 hours.

🐾 - *Appletreewick - Howarth Farm - Middle Skyreholme - Skyreholme Beck - Hell Hole - Height Lathe - Appletreewick.*

📋 *1:25,000 Outdoor leisure Map No. 10 - Yorkshire Dales - Southern area.*

🅿️ - *None. Roadside parking in Appletreewick.*

🍷 - *Craven Arms and New Inn, Appletreewick. Teas at cottage at entrance to Parcevall Hall.*

ABOUT THE WALK - Appletreewick is a particularly attractive village with old hall and stocks, and well worth wandering around. The walk takes you into stunning limestone countryside around Skyreholme Beck and onto a swallow hole. You return over the fields with distant views. You have the option of visiting Parcevall Hall Gardens on the way and visiting Trollers Gill an impressive limestone gorge. If you are camping in the area this walk serves as a good introduction to the opportunites that exist.

WALKING INSTRUCTIONS - Starting from the church dedicated to St. John the Baptist in Appletreewick, opposite High Hall is the path and sign - New Road. The path goes eastwards across the numerous fields and is well stiled - more than ten in 1/2 mile! Reaching the road turn right and descend a short distance before turning left along the lane past Howarth Farm and in 1/2 mile the road junction opposite the telephone kiosk in Middle Skyreholme. Follow the lane to your right and turn left in a few yards at the stile and path sign - Parcevall Hall. Head north and cross three fields to the entrance to the hall and tearoom. Turn left then right at a gate and path sign - New Road 1 mile. Keep Skyreholme Beck on your right for 1/2 mile to a fork in the dale. To your right 1/4 mile away is Trollers Gill. Turn left and begin ascending passing Middle Hill on your right. In 1/2 mile reach a stile. Follow the track beyond looping round to your left for 150 yards to a swallow Hole - Hell Hole - on your left. Turn left past it and follow a faint path to New Road. Turn left to the lefthand bend in the road. Turn left along it for 50 yards to a gate, track and path sign - Hartlington 1 3/

continued opposite.

AIRTON, KIRBY MALHAM & THE PENNINE WAY - 4 1/2 MILES

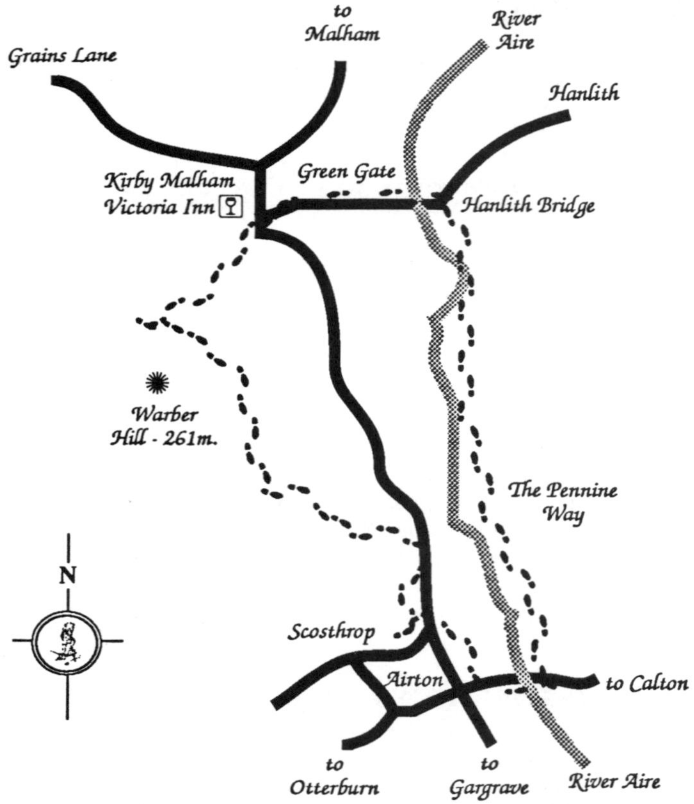

Airton and River Aire.

AIRTON, KIRKBY MALHAM & THE PENNINE WAY - 4 1/2 MILES
- allow 2 hours.

- Airton - River Aire - Pennine Way - Hanlith Bridge - Kirkby Malham - Warber Hill - Scosthrop - Airton.

1:25,000 Outdoor Leisure Map No. 10 - Yorkshire Dales - Southern area.

- No official one - roadside parking in Airton.

- Victoria Inn, Kirkby Malham.

ABOUT THE WALK - Since the fabled Pennine Way meanders through the Dales, at least one walk had to include a section of it - this is it! Nearly half the walk is along it near the River Aire before leaving the way and entering Kirkby Malham, with an inn! You return over Warber Hill and descend back to Airton. A beautiful walk in classic dale scenery.

WALKING INSTRUCTIONS - From Airton descend to the bridge over the River Aire and the Pennine Way. Go through the stile and head northwards along the defined path with the river on your left. Keep on this path for the next 1 1/2 miles to Hanlith Bridge and the minor road between Hanlith and Kirby Malham. Turn left along the road - Green Gate - to Kirby Malham and the Victoria Inn. Cross the Malham road and continue past the church dedicated to St. Michael. Almost opposite the church turn left as footpath signed - Otterburn 2 3/4 miles. Cross a footbridge and ascend diagonally to your right, guided by stiles and keep to the lefthand side of a small wood in less than 1/4 mile. Ascend a large field beyond to a stile and after this keep a wall on your left for a few yards to a gate and footpath sign - Airton 1/2 mile. Just infront is the summit of Warber Hill. Turn left and follow the path around the base of the hill, keeping a wall on your left most of the time. In less than 1/2 mile at the third stile turn left, keeping the wall on your left, and descend diagonally to your right and using several gates to reach the Malham road. Here turn right immediately at the stile and path sign - Scosthrop 1/4 mile. The path keeps to the righthand side of the fields and you gain Scosthrop, part of Airton. Turn left at the minor road then right along the Malham road for a few yards back into central Airton.

WINTERBURN & WINTERBURN RESERVOIR - 5 1/2 MILES

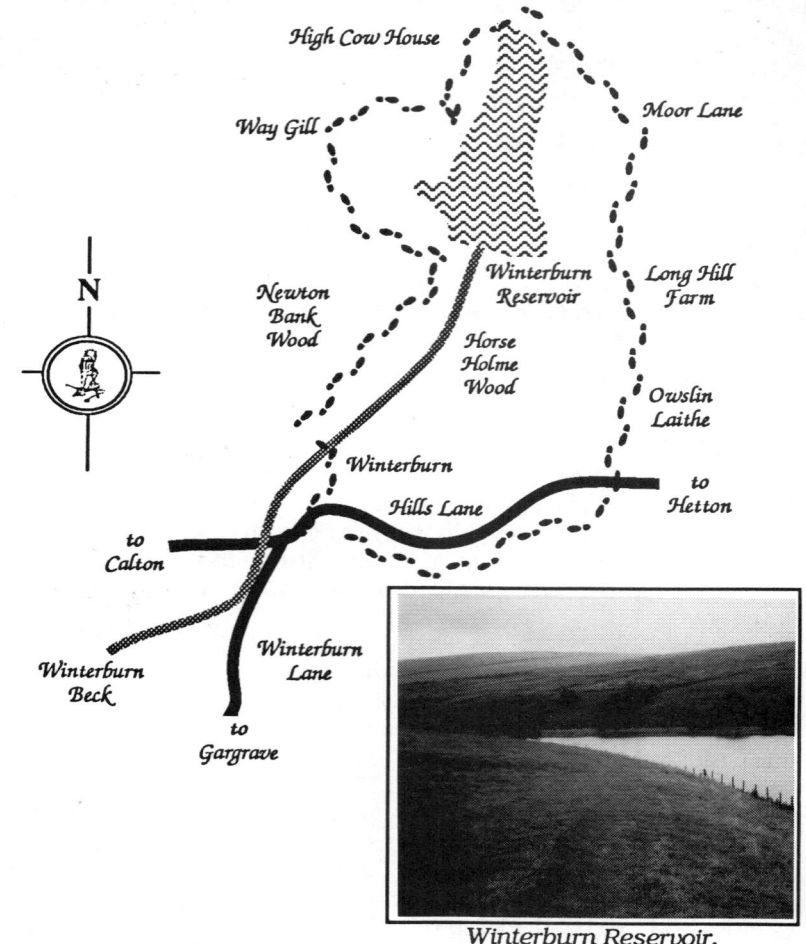

Winterburn Reservoir.

from opposite page -
another footpath junction 1/4 mile away. Here at Moor Lane, turn right as footpath signed - Winterburn. Soon reach a stile and Alans Plantation. Continue to Long Hill Farm 1/4 mile away. Here you leave the reservoir far too your right and go through a gate by a footpath sign and gently ascend and descend open countryside on a faint path to Owslin Laithe approx 1/3 mile away. Keep the wall on your left to a gate and onto Hills Lane, reached beside a bridlepath sign - Moor Lane 1 1/2 miles. Gently descend Hills Lane back to Winterburn Beck where you began.

WINTERBURN & WINTERBURN RESERVOIR - 5 1/2 MILES
- allow 2 hours.

👣 - Winterburn - Winterburn Wood Farm - Way Gill - High Cow House - Winterburn Reservoir - Long Hill Farm - Owslin Laithe - Hills Lane - Winterburn.

🗺️ - 1:25,000 Outdoor Leisure Map - No. 10 - Yorkshire Dales - Southern area.

🅿️ - No official one - roadside parking near Winterburn Beck. Grid Ref. 586934.

🍷 - None on the walk; nearest at Hetton 2 miles to east.

ABOUT THE WALK - A pleasant picturesque and secluded walk up a small valley to Winterburn Reservoir. You get extensive views over the reservoir from both sides as you return high above it to Hills Lane. Parking is restrictive in the area being a narrow lane. The walk is done clockwise.

WALKING INSTRUCTIONS - From the bridge over Winterburn Beck walk up the lane for a few yards to the small road on your left into Winterburn. Cross a cattle-grid and pass a path sign - Way Gill 1 mile - and continue on the road and cross the beck. Just afterwards keep to the right beside the beck and follow the tarmaced road through woodland - Newton Bank Wood on your left; Horse Holme Wood on your right. Follow the road for over 1/2 mile to the reservoir embankment. Here turn left, as footpath signed - Way Gill & High Cow House - still on the tarmaced road. Follow it round woodland and then to your right to Way Gill farm. Here go through the gate on the far right and follow the path down to a stile and tarmaced road. Turn left along it for 200 yards towards High Close Farm, but leave the road at the footpath sign and stile on your right and walk towards the reservoir before turning left and walking close to it guided by stiles. At the end of the reservoir cross a ladder stile and gain woodland and path junction. Turn right over the footbridge and right again, following a defined path/track to

- continued opposite.

RYLSTONE & CRACOE FELL - 6 1/2 MILES

Obelisk

Cross

- from opposite page.

and gate. The path is not defined. Here gain a track - Fell Lane - and follow it for 1/2 mile to the B6265 road at Cracoe. Turn left along it past the Devonshire Arms to the village outskirts where turn left at a gate and follow the bridlepath to Rylstone. The track - Chapel Lane - is well defined and little over 1/2 mile you are back at Rylstone church; all the time the views to the obelisk and cross are on your left.

RYLSTONE & CRACOE FELL
- 6 1/2 MILES
- allow 2 1/2 hours.

🚶🚶🚶 - *Rylstone - Bark Brow - Sun Moor Hill - Cross - Watt Crag Obelisk - Cracoe Fell - Fell Lane (Track) - Cracoe - Chapel Lane (Track) - Rylstone.*

📖 *1:25,000 Outdoor Leisure Map No. 10 - Yorkshire Dales - Southern Area.*

🅿️ - *Beside the B6265 at Rylstone. Grid Ref. 969588.*

🍷 - *Devonshire Arms, Cracoe.*

ABOUT THE WALK - A superb fell walk! Starting from the hamlet of Rylstone, whose church is well worth exploring, you ascend to the moorland and the impressive cross on Sun Moor Hill. Keeping to the edge of the fell you gain Watt Crag and its obelisk. Just afterwards you descend steeply to Fell Lane and gain Cracoe where there is an inn. To return to Rylstone you follow another lane to its church and retrace your steps back to the B6265.

WALKING INSTRUCTIONS - From the B6265 road at Rylstone, walk down the road a few yards before turning left up the lane to Rylstone church, dedicated to St. Peter. Just past the church turn right - you will be returning to here on your way back - as footpath signed - Barden Moor. The is defined and stiled and cross two large fields over the next 1/2 mile to two ladder stiles; on the skyline can be seen the cross, your first destination. After the second ladder stile gain a track. Walk up it for 200 yards to a gate and sign Halton Height. The path is undefined at first but aim for the righthand side of a small plantation, ascending moorland. Just beyond it gain a track and reach a stile. To your right can be seen the remains of Norton Tower. Continue ascending a few more yards to near the crest of the fell before turning left on a path towards the cross. At first you keep a wall on your right to the cross. Afterwards as you head for the obelisk, little over a mile away, keep the wall on your left. Shortly after the obelisk descend the steep slopes diagonally to your right before bearing left to a sheep pen

continued opposite.

HOWGILL & SIMON'S SEAT - 485m. - 4 MILES

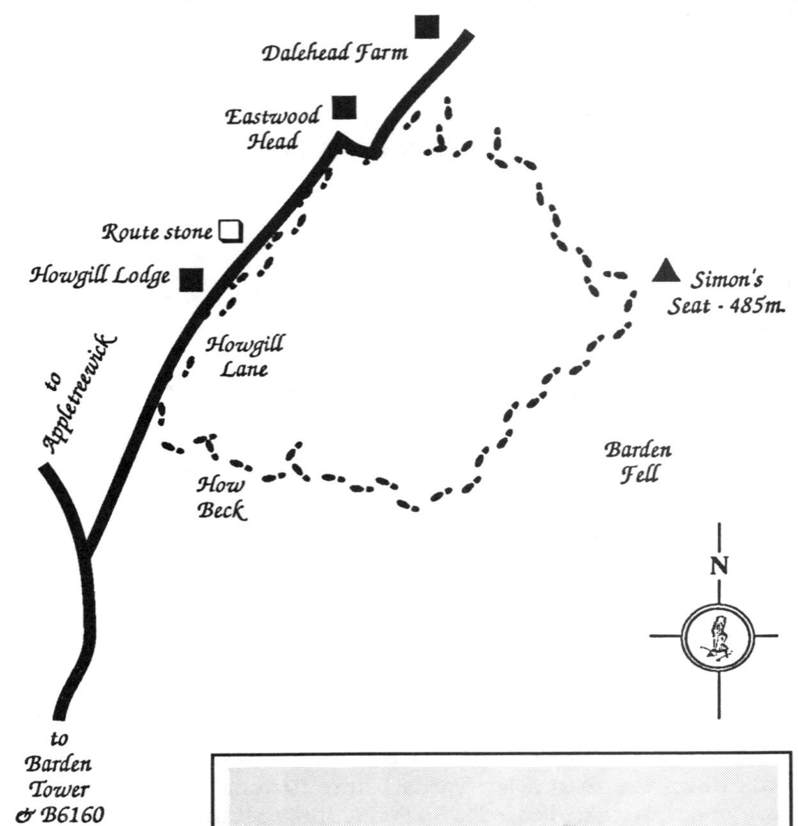

Simon's Seat - 485m.

HOWGILL & SIMON'S SEAT - 485m. - 4 MILES
- allow 1 1/2 hours.

🐾 🐾 🐾 Howgill - Howgill Lane - Eastwood Head - Dalehead Farm - Simon's Seat - How Beck - Howgill.

🗺️ - 1:25,000 Outdoor Leisure Map No. 10 - Yorkshire Dales - Southern Area.

🚗 - Very limited parking on Howgill Lane. Small parking area at How Beck - Grid Ref. 064592.

🍷 - None. Nearest at Appletreewick, just over a mile away. Restaurant at Howgill Lodge (camping & caravaning.)

ABOUT THE WALK - For much of the exploration of the walks in this book I camped at Howgill Lodge, so it is only fitting that one should start from here! The ascent to the gritstone outcrop - Simon's Seat on Barden Fell is very rewarding with magnificent views over Wharfedale and rolling moorland. The bilberries were out and curlew were both seen and heard. Shooting takes place here in the grouse season, so check the moor isn't closed!

WALKING INSTRUCTIONS - Follow the lane - a track - past Howgill Lodge. Just after on your left is an old route sign - "To Patley Bridge." Continue through Eastwood Head, 1/2 mile later and 1/4 mile later before reaching Dalehead Farm, turn right up a zig-zag path. In 1/2 mile this brings you to a ladder stile and the boundary of Access Land. Bear right on the path ascending moorland to the base of the rocks of Simon's Seat. Turn left and ascend to the trig point on the rocks. Before getting there notice the path on your right on the moor - this is your route after the summit. Follow the path along the moor and soon start gently descending to a wall and access point. Turn right and descend a track through woodland on the left of How Beck. At the bottom is Howgill Lane, along which you started the walk.

FLASBY & SHARP HAW - 357M. - 6 MILES

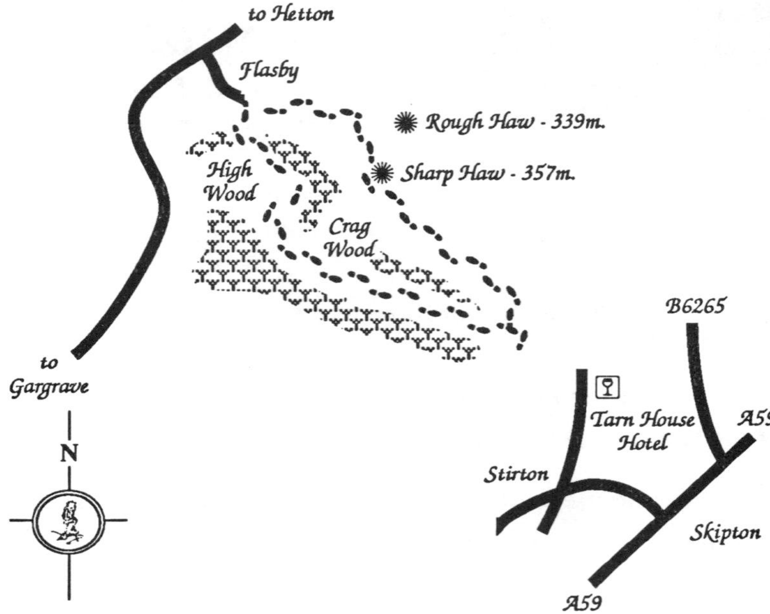

Flasby.

30

FLASBY AND SHARP HAW, 357m.
- 6 MILES
- allow 2 1/2 hours.

- *Flasby - High Wood - Crag Wood - Moorland - Sharp Haw - Flasby.*

1:25,000 Outdoor Leisure Map No. 10 - Yorkshire Dales - Southern Area.

- Roadside parking only in Flasby. Grid Ref. 947567.

- None - nearest at Gargrave or Tarn House Hotel 1/2 mile from route.

ABOUT THE WALK - A remote moorland and woodland walk on good paths. The summit of Sharp Haw is a magnificent vantage point over the southern end of the Yorkshire Dales. There is limited parking at Flasby and the nearest inn is little over 1/2 mile from route. You will see few people just skylarks above.

WALKING INSTRUCTIONS - Walk along the no through road in Flasby past the farms and over the Flasby Beck. Just after turn right at the footpath sign - "Stirton". The path crosses two fields to a track, where turn left, heading towards High Wood. Go through a gate and follow the curving track to the wood and a kissing gate. Continue on the track and remain on it through the woodland for the next 1 1/2 miles, heading south-east; en route passing a footpath sign - "Bog Lane 1 1/2 miles." After a mile you will see a rocky escarpment on your left. At the end of the wood reach a gate and stile. Continue on the track in open countryside for another 1/4 mile to a bridlepath sign. Turn left and follow the grass track to a gate and on towards Sharp Low. Bear left on a path and ascend the hill gained after a ladder stile. Leave the summit on its right and descend a path to a stile and path in the saddle between Sharp Haw and Rough Hay. Turn left along this path which descends steadily to the right of woodland and in a mile reach a gate and a track. Continue on the track and little over 1/4 mile you are back in Flasby with your starting out path on your left.

BOLTON PRIORY - 7 1/2 MILES

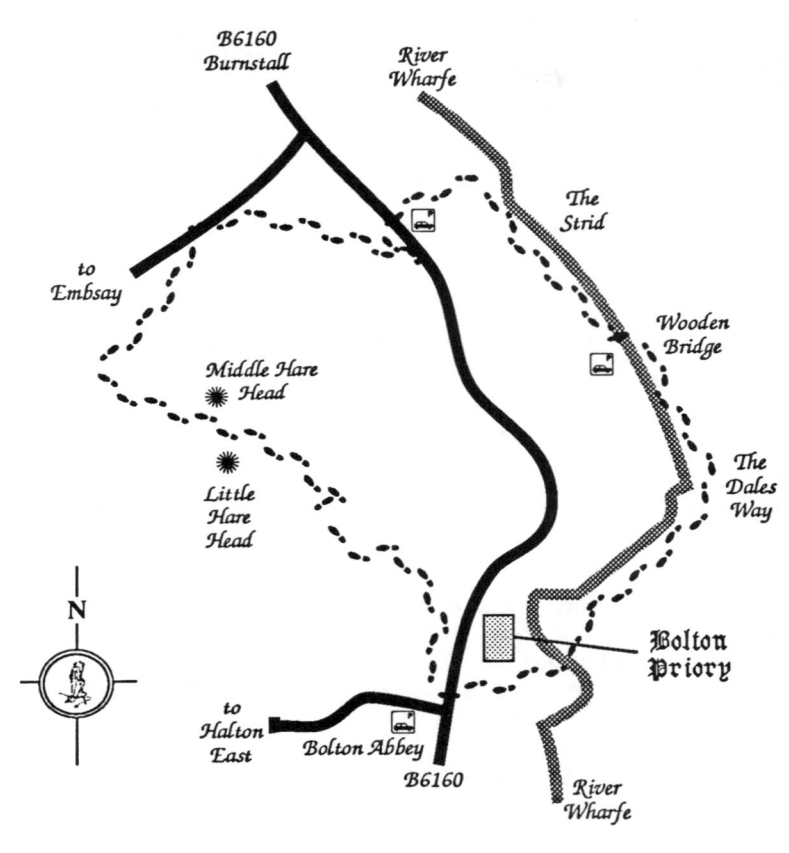

from opposite page -
Walk past the cottages and in 1/4 mile gain The Dales Way and bear right along it. Soon you pass the narrow river channel - The Strid. Continue for nearly 2 miles with the River Wharfe on your left back to Wooden Bridge where you began.

BOLTON PRIORY - The present ruins date back to 1150 being founded by Augustinian Monks of the Cistercian Order. With the dissolution of the monasteries the priory ceased in 1538. The area including Bolton Hall are part of the Duke Of Devonshire Yorkshire estate. The stone arch over the road was built by the monks to bring water into the Priory to drive their flour mill.

BOLTON PRIORY - 7 1/2 MILES
- allow 3 hours.

 - Wooden Bridge Car Park - River Wharfe - Bolton Priory - Little Hare Head - Hare Head Side - Barden Beck - B6160 - Strid Cottage - Dales Way - River Wharfe - Wooden Bridge.

1:25,000 Outdoor Leisure Map No. 10 - Yorkshire Dales - Southern area.

- Wooden Bridge, Grid Ref. 078553. Others at Grid Ref. 058565 and 072539.

Tearoom at Bolton Priory and Wooden Bridge.

ABOUT THE WALK - The longest in the book but an outstanding one! Starting with delightful walking beside the River Wharfe to the ruined Bolton Priory. From here you cross moorland on good paths before returning to the river and a two mile stretch back to your start.

WALKING INSTRUCTIONS - From the car park at Wooden Bridge, cross the river and turn right, signposted path - Bolton Priory 1 mile - part of The Dales Way. You keep close to the river to a ford and road in 1/4 mile, before continuing near the river and across a bridge to the Priory. Keep to the left of it to reach the B6160 road. Turn right and walk under the road arch and few yards later turn left at a stile and follow a track. It curves round to your right then left to gates and woodland. Here is a bridlepath sign - Halton Height. Keep on the track through the woodland, looping to your left and guided by bridlepath signs. At the end of the wood gain a gate and continue in open country to a stile 1/4 mile away. Much of the route is marked by blue paint on the boulders. Continue across the next field to the top lefthand corner where there is a stile and bridlepath sign. Here bear left and keep a wall on your left for the next 1/2 mile, passing inbetween Little Hare Head and Middle Hare Head. Bear right to another wall which keep on your left to gain a gate in a wall. Continue a few more yards before turning right and descending the path to a stile and minor road, beside path sign - "Halton East." Turn right and in a few yards right at a stile and path sign - "to B6160 1 miles." Follow a track for a few yards before bearing left at a stile and path sign. The pathline is faint but you contour round the slope to a wall 1/2 mile away. Keep the wall on your left for 1/4 mile before leaving it and continuing ahead to the B6160 road. Turn left and in 100 yards right into the Bolton Priory estate.

continued opposite -

EMBASY MOOR RESERVOIR AND CRAG - 3 1/2 MILES

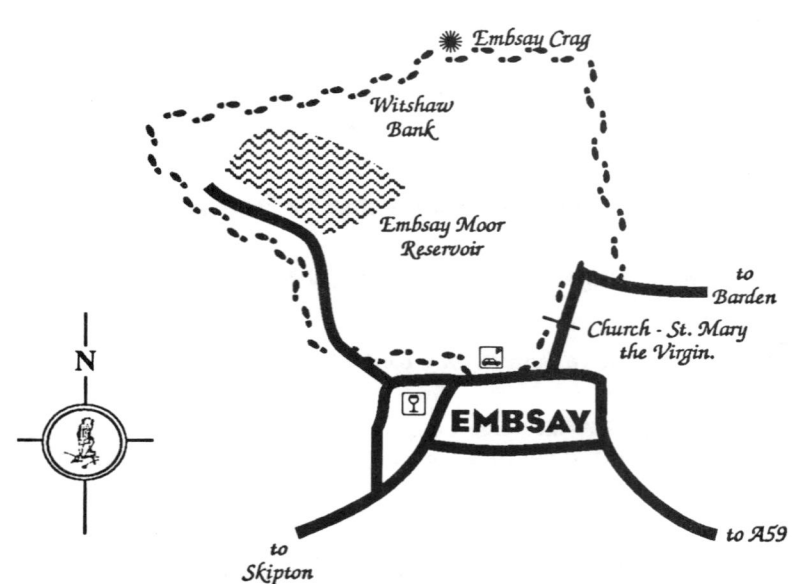

Embsay Moor Reservoir and Crag.

EMBSAY MOOR RESERVOIR AND CRAG - 3 1/2 MILES
- allow 1 1/2 hours.

 - Embsay - Embsay Moor Reservoir - Witshaw Bank - Embsay Crag - Embsay Kirk - Embsay.

 - 1:25,000 Outdoor Leisure Map No. 10 - Yorkshire Dales - southern area.

Embsay village - Grid Ref. 009538

- Embsay.

ABOUT THE WALK - A short stunning walk around a reservoir before ascending to the summit of Embsay Crag. The whole area is photogenic! A pleasant contrast of moorland, lofty summit and rippling water.

WALKING INSTRUCTIONS - At the back of the car park is the stile and path. Over the stile turn left - you will be retuning from the right. The path goes around the houses to the reservoir road. Turn right along the road and in 1/2 mile near the reservoir is a footpath sign - "Embsay Crag 1 mile." Continue on the road around the lefthand side of the reservoir to a stile beyond the reservoir. Turn right along the track first above the reservoir and in 1/4 mile turn left and ascend the path up Witshaw Bank to the summit of Embsay Crag. Walk above the crag before descending to a gate. Turn right and continue descending to a stile and track on the left of woodland. Continue down the track to the road and turn right along it following it round to your left, passing Embsay Kirk. Pass the church dedicated to St. Mary the Virgin and just afterwards turn right and follow the path back to the car park in central Embsay.

SETTLE & ATTERMIRE SCAR - 5 MILES

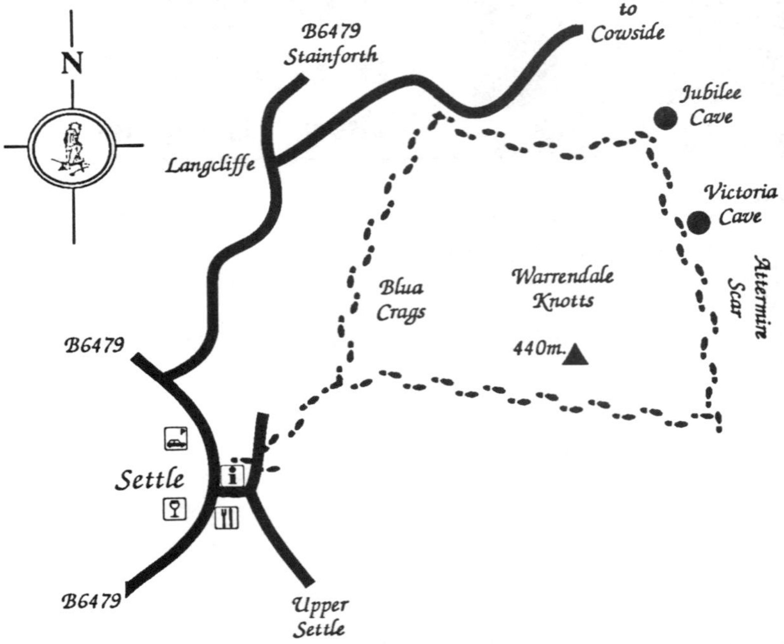

Attermire Scar and view to Victoria Cave.

SETTLE & ATTERMIRE SCAR
- 5 MILES
- allow 2 hours

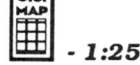 - Settle - Attermire Cave - Attermire Scar - Victoria Cave - Jubilee Cave - Blua Crags - Settle.

 - 1:25,000 Outdoor Leisure map No. 10 - Yorkshire Dales - Southern area.

 - Central Settle.

- Several in Settle & tearooms.

ABOUT THE WALK - A truly excellent walk through the limestone scenery to the impressive Attermire Scar. There are several caves to explore before descending your way back with extensive views over Settle.

WALKING INSTRUCTIONS - From the square beside the Town Hall and Information Centre, exit from the top lefthand corner. Follow the road round to your right then left. In a few yards leave it and ascend the walled track heading for Langcliffe - you will return down this track at the end. Follow it for 1/4 mile to the signed path for Malham. Turn right and ascend more steeply, soon keeping a wall on your left as you head due east. Little over 1/4 mile reach a stile. Keep left with a wall on your immediate left. In 1/4 mile bear right and keep the wall on your right to reach a ladder stile. Descend and pass a ruined building on your left and in a few more yards to near the base of Attermire Scar. Turn left to a ladder stile and follow the defined path beneath the scar for the next mile; enroute passing Victoria Cave up to your right after 2/3 mile. Keep a wall on your left and ascend stiles to gain a track. Continue along it to a ladder stile; to your right is Jubilee Cave. Turn left over the stile and descend the large field; the pathline is faint. At the end of the bottom righthand corner of the field is a track and cattle grid. Turn right and descend to the road from Langcliffe. A few yards down it turn left at a gate and path sign - Settle 1 1/4 miles. The path is defined and well gated as you contour round the slopes gradually descending. In a mile reach the path to Malham you took earlier. Retrace your steps down to Settle.

BEAMSLEY BEACON, 393m. - 2 MILES

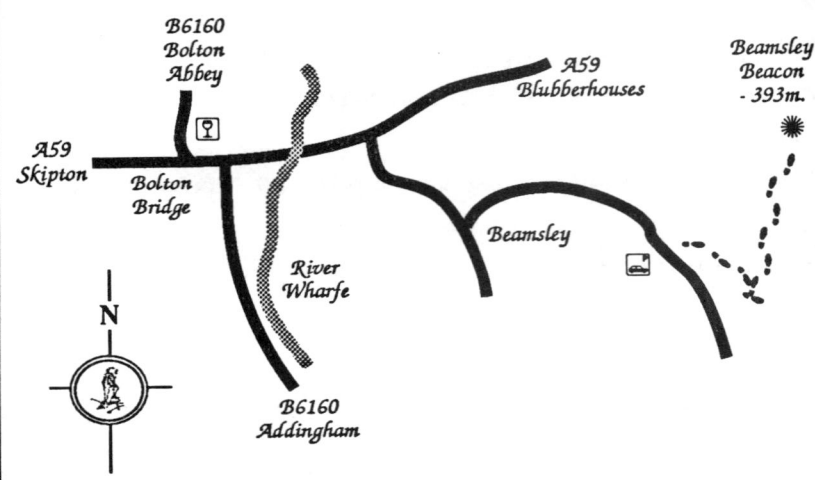

Beamsley Beacon - 393m.

BEAMSLEY BEACON - 2 MILES
- allow 40 minutes.

- Howber Hill Farm - Beamsley Beacon and return.

1:25,000 Outdoor Leisure map - No. 10 - Yorkshire Dales - southern area.

- near Howber Hill Farm. Grid Ref. 093522.

- None. Nearest at Bolton Bridge.

ABOUT THE WALK - A very short return walk to the summit of Beamsley Beacon, 393m. The views from its summit over the southern half of the Yorkshire Dales is stunning; especially looking north up Wharfedale. As you approach the dales along the A59 the beacon stands out asking to be ascended! I answered its call and hope you too divert to here and enjoy this high secluded spot.

WALKING INSTRUCTIONS - From the car park cross the road and ascend the grass path beside the wall to the ridge. Here turn left for the summit 1/2 mile away. Return the same way.

LEEDS & LIVERPOOL CANAL

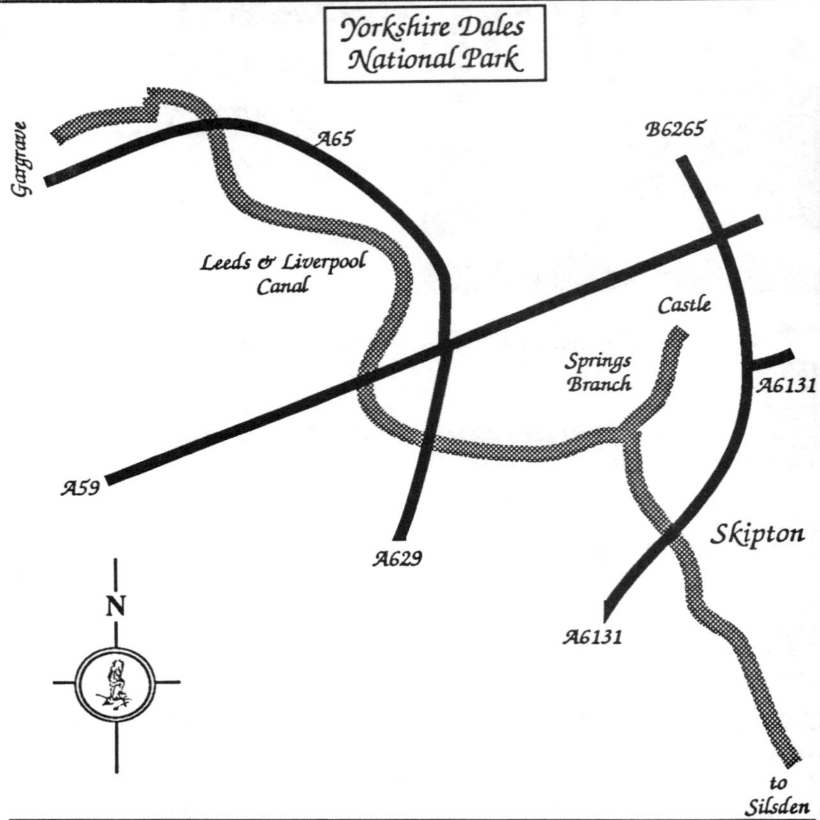

Leeds & Liverpool Canal in Skipton.

LEEDS & LIVERPOOL CANAL - 3 WALKS.

1. Skipton to Gargrave - 5 miles one way.
2. Skipton - Springs branch - 1 mile
3. Skipton - Silsden - 6 1/2 miles one way.

 - 1:25,000 Outdoor leisure Map No. 10 - Yorkshire Dales - Southern area.

Central Skipton.

- Numerous in Skipton and Gargrave. One at Silsden.

ABOUT THE WALKS - While just outside the National Park, the canal does have magnificent walking along its towpaths. The walk along the canal from Skipton to Gargrave is basically along the edge of the park. Starting from the canal junction in Skipton you can do the short walk up the Springs branch into a ravine and the ramparts of Skipton Castle. The walk south to Silsden is one totally away from the bustle of modern life. The one to Gargrave is to a picturesque location. The choice of routes is yours! All have well defined towpaths to follow.

THE LEEDS & LIVERPOOL CANAL - At 127 miles long it is the longest single canal built by one company. Started in 1770 it took forty years at a cost of over £1.2 million before it was complete. Along its route are 91 locks.

Leeds & Liverpool Canal in Skipton.

WALK RECORD CHART

Date walked -

GRIMWITH RESERVOIR - 4 MILES ....

KILNSEY CRAG - 2 1/2 MILES ....

STAINFORTH & CATRIGG FORCE - 3 MILES ....

BORDLEY - 5 MILES ....

MALHAM COVE - 5 MILES ....

GRASSINGTON - 5 MILES ....

APPLETREEWICK - 4 1/2 MILES ....

AIRTON - 4 1/2 MILES ....

WINTERBURN - 5 1/2 MILES ....

RYLSTONE - 6 1/2 MILES ....

HOWGILL & SIMON'S SEAT - 4 MILES ....

FLASBY & SHARP HAW - 357m - 6 MILES ....

BOLTON PRIORY - 7 1/2 MILES..

EMBSAY MOOR RESERVOIR & CRAG - 3 1/2 MILES ....

SETTLE & ATTERMIRE SCAR - 5 MILES ....

BEAMSLEY BEACON, 393m. - 2 MILES ....

LEEDS & LIVERPOOL CANAL - 3 WALKS ....

THE JOHN MERRILL'S WALK BADGE

Complete six of the walks in this book and get the above special John Merrill walk badge. and signed certificate. Badges are a black cloth with walking man embroidered in four colours and measure - 3 1/2" in diameter.

BADGE ORDER FORM

Date and details of walks completed..

....

NAME ....

ADDRESS ....

....

Price: £2.75 each including postage, VAT and signed completion certificate.
Amount enclosed (Payable to Trail Crest Publications) ..
            From: TRAIL CREST PUBLICATIONS Ltd.,
           Winster, Matlock, Derbyshire. DE4 2DQ.

℗ /**Fax** (0629) 826354 - 24hr answering service.

************* YOU MAY PHOTOCOPY THIS FORM *********

"I'VE DONE A JOHN MERRILL WALK" T SHIRT -

Emerald Green with white lettering and walking man logo. Send £7.50 to Trail Crest Publications stating size required.

REMEMBER AND OBSERVE THE COUNTRY CODE

Enjoy the countryside and respect its life and work.

Guard against all risk of fire.

Fasten all gates.

Keep your dogs under close control.

Keep to public paths across farmland.

Use gates and stiles to cross fences, hedges and walls.

Leave livestock, crops and machinery alone.

Take your litter home - pack it in; pack it out.

Help to keep all water clean.

Protect wildlife, plants and trees.

Take special care on country roads

Make no unnecessary noise.

THE HIKER'S CODE

❀ Hike only along marked routes - do not leave the trail.

❀ Use stiles to climb fences; close gates.

❀ Camp only in designated campsites.

❀ Carry a light-weight stove.

❀ Leave the trail cleaner than you found it.

❀ Leave flowers and plants for others to enjoy.

❀ Keep dogs on a leash.

❀ Protect and do not disturb wildlife.

❀ Use the trail at your own risk.

❀ Leave only your thanks and footprints - take nothing but photographs.

EQUIPMENT NOTES
.... some personal thoughts

BOOTS - *preferably with a full leather upper, of medium weight, with a vibram sole. I always add a foam cushioned insole to help cushion the base of my feet.*

SOCKS - *I generally wear two thick pairs as this helps minimise blisters. The inner pair are of loop stitch variety and approximately 80% wool. The outer are a thick rib pair of approximately 80% wool.*

WATERPROOFS - *for general walking I wear a T shirt or cotton shirt with a cotton wind jacket on top. You generate heat as you walk and I prefer to layer my clothes to avoid getting too hot. Depending on the season will dictate how many layers you wear. In soft rain I just use my wind jacket for I know it quickly dries out. In heavy or consistant rain I slip on a neoprene lined cagoule, and although hot and clammy it does keep me reasonably dry. Only in extreme conditions will I don overtrousers, much preferring to get wet and feel comfortable. I never wear gaiters!*

FOOD - *as I walk I carry bars of chocolate, for they provide instant energy and are light to carry. In winter a flask of hot coffee is welcome. I never carry water and find no hardship from not doing so, but this is a personal matter! From experience I find the more I drink the more I want and sweat. You should always carry some extra food such as Kendal Mint Cake, for emergencies.*

RUCKSACKS - *for day walking I use a climbing rucksack of about 40 litre capacity and although it leaves excess space it does mean that the sac is well padded, with an internal frame and padded shoulder straps. Inside apart from the basics for one day I carry gloves, balaclava, spare pullover and a pair of socks.*

MAP & COMPASS - *when I am walking I always have the relevant map - preferably 1:25,000 scale - open in my hand. This enables me to constantly check that I am walking the right way. In case of bad weather I carry a compass, which once mastered gives you complete confidence in thick cloud or mist.*

"from footprint to finished book"

OTHER BOOKS by John N. Merrill Published by TRAIL CREST PUBLICATIONS Ltd.

CIRCULAR WALK GUIDES -
SHORT CIRCULAR WALKS IN THE PEAK DISTRICT - Vol. 1 and 2
CIRCULAR WALKS IN WESTERN PEAKLAND
SHORT CIRCULAR WALKS IN THE STAFFORDSHIRE MOORLANDS
SHORT CIRCULAR WALKS - TOWNS & VILLAGES OF THE PEAK DISTRICT
SHORT CIRCULAR WALKS AROUND MATLOCK
SHORT CIRCULAR WALKS IN THE DUKERIES
SHORT CIRCULAR WALKS IN SOUTH YORKSHIRE
SHORT CIRCULAR WALKS IN SOUTH DERBYSHIRE
SHORT CIRCULAR WALKS AROUND BUXTON
SHORT CIRCULAR WALKS AROUND WIRKSWORTH
SHORT CIRCULAR WALKS IN THE HOPE VALLEY
40 SHORT CIRCULAR WALKS IN THE PEAK DISTRICT
CIRCULAR WALKS ON KINDER & BLEAKLOW
SHORT CIRCULAR WALKS IN SOUTH NOTTINGHAMSHIRE
SHIRT CIRCULAR WALKS IN CHESHIRE
SHORT CIRCULAR WALKS IN WEST YORKSHIRE
CIRCULAR WALKS TO PEAK DISTRICT AIRCRAFT WRECKS by John Mason
CIRCULAR WALKS IN THE DERBYSHIRE DALES
SHORT CIRCULAR WALKS IN EAST DEVON
SHORT CIRCULAR WALKS AROUND HARROGATE
SHORT CIRCULAR WALKS IN CHARNWOOD FOREST
SHORT CIRCULAR WALKS AROUND CHESTERFIELD
SHORT CIRCULAR WALKS IN THE YORKS DALES - Vol 1 - Southern area.
LONG CIRCULAR WALKS IN THE PEAK DISTRICT - Vol.1 and 2.
LONG CIRCULAR WALKS IN THE STAFFORDSHIRE MOORLANDS
WALKING THE TISSINGTON TRAIL
WALKING THE HIGH PEAK TRAIL

CANAL WALKS -
VOL 1 - DERBYSHIRE & NOTTINGHAMSHIRE
VOL 2 - CHESHIRE & STAFFORDSHIRE
VOL 3 - STAFFORDSHIRE
VOL 4 - THE CHESHIRE RING
VOL 5 - LINCOLNSHIRE & NOTTINGHAMSHIRE
VOL 6 - SOUTH YORKSHIRE
VOL 7 - THE TRENT & MERSEY CANAL

JOHN MERRILL DAY CHALLENGE WALKS -
WHITE PEAK CHALLENGE WALK
DARK PEAK CHALLENGE WALK
PEAK DISTRICT END TO END WALKS
STAFFORDSHIRE MOORLANDS CHALLENGE WALK
THE LITTLE JOHN CHALLENGE WALK
YORKSHIRE DALES CHALLENGE WALK
NORTH YORKSHIRE MOORS CHALLENGE WALK
LAKELAND CHALLENGE WALK

THE RUTLAND WATER CHALLENGE WALK
MALVERN HILLS CHALLENGE WALK
THE SALTER'S WAY
THE SNOWDON CHALLENGE
CHARNWOOD FOREST CHALLENGE WALK
THREE COUNTIES CHALLENGE WALK (Peak District).

INSTRUCTION & RECORD -
HIKE TO BE FIT.....STROLLING WITH JOHN
THE JOHN MERRILL WALK RECORD BOOK

MULTIPLE DAY WALKS -
THE RIVERS'S WAY
PEAK DISTRICT: HIGH LEVEL ROUTE
PEAK DISTRICT MARATHONS
THE LIMEY WAY
THE PEAKLAND WAY

COAST WALKS & NATIONAL TRAILS -
ISLE OF WIGHT COAST PATH
PEMBROKESHIRE COAST PATH
THE CLEVELAND WAY

PEAK DISTRICT HISTORICAL GUIDES -
A to Z GUIDE OF THE PEAK DISTRICT
DERBYSHIRE INNS - an A to Z guide
HALLS AND CASTLES OF THE PEAK DISTRICT & DERBYSHIRE
TOURING THE PEAK DISTRICT & DERBYSHIRE BY CAR
DERBYSHIRE FOLKLORE
PUNISHMENT IN DERBYSHIRE
CUSTOMS OF THE PEAK DISTRICT & DERBYSHIRE
WINSTER - a souvenir guide
ARKWRIGHT OF CROMFORD
LEGENDS OF DERBYSHIRE
TALES FROM THE MINES by Geoffrey Carr
PEAK DISTRICT PLACE NAMES by Martin Spray

JOHN MERRILL'S MAJOR WALKS -
TURN RIGHT AT LAND'S END
WITH MUSTARD ON MY BACK
TURN RIGHT AT DEATH VALLEY
EMERALD COAST WALK

SKETCH BOOKS -
SKETCHES OF THE PEAK DISTRICT

OVERSEAS GUIDES -
HIKING IN NEW MEXICO - Vol I - The Sandia and Manzano Mountains.
Vol 2 - Hiking "Billy the Kid" Country.
"WALKING IN DRACULA COUNTRY" - Romania.

IN PREPARATION -
SHORT CIRCULAR WALKS IN EAST STAFFORDSHIRE
SHORT CIRCULAR WALKS IN THE AMBER VALLEY (DERBYSHIRE).
LONG CIRCULAR WALKS IN CHESHIRE

for a copy
of the
**John Merrill
Walk Guide**
Catalogue
write to -
Trail Crest Publications Ltd.,
Milne House, Speedwell Mill,
Miller's Green, Wirksworth,
Derbyshire. DE4 4BL